W9-CNQ-829

ESSENTIAL MARTIAL ARTS

Written by Simon Mugford
Designed by Barry Green and the Top That! Team

Tangerine Press®

Copyright © 2002 Top That! Publishing plc
Published by Tangerine Press, an imprint of Scholastic Inc.
557 Broadway, New York, NY 10012.
Scholastic and Tangerine Press and associated logos are trademarks of Scholastic Inc.
Printed and bound in China

The word "martial" means war-like, and the first martial artists developed their skills for use in battle.

Arts and Aims

Becoming a good martial artist takes years of practice, mental training and self-discipline. It is not simply about being able to defeat an opponent.

Asian Origins

The many forms of martial arts originated hundreds of years ago in Asia. China, Japan, Korea and Thailand produced most of the best-known styles.

The ancient art of t'ai chi is a gentle, yet powerful, martial art.

World Sports

Martial arts are now extremely popular all over the world. Most disciplines have world championship competitions, while tae kwon do and judo are both represented at the Olympic Games.

Screen Stars

Since the 1970s, martial arts movies have helped to increase the popularity of certain styles. Kung fu expert Bruce Lee is probably the best-known of the martial arts movie stars.

Martial Arts Philosophy

Although many martial arts may appear to be aggressive, in reality their practice is based upon a thoughtful and philosophical approach.

Anti-Anger
Self-discipline, courtesy and respect for others are central to all martial arts. The belief is that through training and study, the martial artist learns to control his or her aggression and becomes a more peaceful person. Martial arts are much more than hobbies; they are a way of life to followers.

Weapons and Moods
Even the styles that use weapons are concerned with bringing the body and mind into harmony. Although they may appear aggressive at first, this is misleading because martial arts are as much about predicting and avoiding conflict as they are about dealing with it when it happens.

Inner Peace
Practicing meditation is believed to help the martial artist find inner peace and control aggression.

Confucianism
The teachings of Confucius — a 6th-century BC teacher and philosopher — influence the practice of many Chinese martial arts. Its main teaching is, "Never do to others what you would not like them to do to you."

Shorinji Kempo
Shorinji kempo is a martial art that has its origins in India more than 5,000 years ago. It is said that the Buddha was so impressed by the art as a way of unifying the mind and body that he incorporated it into his teachings. Today there are many forms of kempo.

The lotus position is used in meditation.

4

Shinto

Many Japanese martial arts are based upon the philosophies of the Shinto religion. Shinto centers on the worship of the gods of nature.

Zen Philosophy

Zen is a type of Japanese Buddhism. Its followers spend long periods of time in deep meditation. This helps to turn the mind away from the distractions of everyday life.

Zen Archery

Kyudo is a Japanese martial art that is a form of archery. It is practiced to increase mental discipline rather than as a sport. The way that the arrow is loaded and released is more important than accuracy.

Kyudo, a martial art which is also a form of archery.

Religion has a key role in the practice, study and teaching of martial arts. Buddhism, which teaches self-discipline and mental awareness, is especially significant.

Spiritual Art

Holy men traveled from India to China, taking the teachings of Buddhism with them. They learned martial arts as a way to defend themselves. To the true martial artist, the spiritual side of the arts is as important as the physical.

Traveling Monks

The Shaolin monks were famous martial artists. They traveled widely throughout Asia, introducing the arts to different countries. Their work continues today, as the monks put on martial arts displays around the world.

The Shaolin Temple.

Shaolin Temple

The Shaolin Temple in China is one of the most important places in the world for martial arts. It is thought to be more than 1,600 years old. Regarded as the ancient center for Chinese kung fu, the buildings spread out over 10,000 acres.

The world-famous Shaolin monks demonstrating their extreme martial arts capabilities.

Taoism

Chinese martial arts are closely linked to the Taoist religion. The yin/yang symbol of Taoism represents how strength is balanced with compassion and gentleness. Unlike other religions, Taoism does not consider good behavior as important as acting in harmony with nature. It is believed that by acting in harmony with nature, good behavior will follow.

A student practicing t'ai chi.

There are many hundreds of styles of martial arts.

Hard and Soft
They can be broadly divided into hard styles — in which punches, kicks and strikes are practiced — and soft styles, which focus on the control of power. Many martial arts combine the two. Broadly, they can also be separated by country, as some martial arts are particularly associated with China, some with Japan, some with the Philippines and others with Korea.

Bowing
Respect for your teacher and opponent is an important part of martial arts. In judo, students must kneel to bow to their teacher before a lesson. Opponents must make a standing bow to one another at the beginning and end of a contest. Bowing is really the equivalent to the ritual of shaking hands that takes place in other sports, such as soccer and tennis.

Clothing
Each martial art has a special kind of clothing. In judo and aikido, the suit is called a judogi; in karate it is called a gi. It is made of heavy cotton, which can withstand a lot of tugging.

The karate uniform worn when training.

Belt

The belt serves two purposes. It holds the jacket in place and the color of the belt indicates the level of skill that the artist has reached. In judo, for example, artists progress from white to black belt. The belt is worn with pride.

Weapons

Many arts involve the use of weapons. Kendo, for instance uses a wooden sword called a shinai. Most beginners will practice the art without weapons.

The bow (zarei) is done from the seiza (kneeling) position.

Weapons have a number of different roles in martial arts. Some styles, such as kendo, are based entirely around the use of a weapon.

Weapon Skills

Martial arts such as kung fu use weapon skills as part of the practice of self-defense. The student is taught to regard the weapon with respect. The study of traditional weapons helps the student to understand the dynamics of his body and how to generate power. The skills developed help to improve performance in the martial arts that don't use weapons.

Basics

In any of the weapon arts, students will learn basic techniques before they begin to handle weapons. This is as much for their own protection as for their opponents'.

Kendo

Kendo is one of the most widely practiced of the weapons arts. It has its origins in the sword-fighting schools of the Japanese samurai. Kendo weapons include tanto, shoto, daito and suburito sticks.

Jedi

Fans of the "Star Wars" films will be familiar with some of the moves of kendo and other Japanese sword-fighting arts. They provided the inspiration for the famous light saber battle scenes.

The Japanese art of kendo.

Nunchakus, swords and kamas are just some of the weapons used in martial arts.

Iaido

Iaido is the art of drawing and attacking with the sword. It is mostly practiced alone. Iaido is a test of imagination and concentration.

Moving Meditation

Weapon arts such as kendo and kyudo (Japanese archery) teach awareness and control of the body. The use of a weapon demands increased concentration, and most martial arts focus on this side, rather than any aggressive use.

Stick Skills

The Filipino martial arts of escrima, arnis and kali teach skills using simple rattan sticks. This has its origins in a period during which the people of the Philippines were banned from owning, or using, weapons.

Weapon arts teach awareness and control of the body.

The so-called empty-hand arts are mainly based on fighting with bare hands and feet.

Karate was little-known in the west until the early part of the 20th century.

King Karate
Karate, one of the most widely practiced of all the martial arts, is the king of the empty-hand styles. The very name karate means "empty-hand." Empty-hand styles are taught as sport and as self-defense.

Karate
Karate began on the Japanese island of Okinawa during the 15th century. At the time, carrying weapons on the island was forbidden, so the people developed alternative ways of protecting themselves.

Four Styles
There are four styles of karate – shotokan, wado ryu, shito ryu, and goju ryu. There are some differences between the styles, but they share the basic principles of high-energy punches, kicks and strikes.

Jujitsu uses throws, locks and holds.

This karate block is a jodan uke (upper block).

Karate Competition

Competitive karate is very fast. A bout will last two or three minutes and points are scored according to technique and striking targets.

Jujitsu

Jujitsu is an ancient Japanese martial art, which uses a series of throws, locks and holds. Its name means "gentle fighting art."

Past and Present

Jujitsu shares some of its roots with the very well-known sport of sumo wrestling and forms the basis of modern judo. It is practiced mainly as a self-defense art.

Many of the great martial arts originated in China. Indeed, the Shaolin monks, considered by many to be the masters of martial arts, were based in northern China.

T'ai chi is an internal martial art.

Influence

The ancient culture, religion and philosophy of this unique country has had an important influence on the world of martial arts.

Origins

According to legend, martial arts were introduced to China by a Buddhist traveling from India in search of enlightenment. He arrived at a monastery where he taught the monks martial arts exercises in an attempt to increase their physical health.

Wai-chia

The term wai-chia refers to the external hard styles of Chinese martial arts. These include some forms of kung fu, jeet kune do and Chinese kickboxing. They are typically fast and aggressive-looking, though still philosophical in outlook.

Kickboxing is now practiced throughout the western world.

Nei-chia

Nei-chia are the internal soft styles. These include t'ai chi, pa kua chang and fusing-i chuan. These are practiced for physical and mental exercise, rather than as competitive sports or self-defense.

T'ai chi requires practicing its principles, not only physically, but also in body and mind.

Kung fu is one of the most widely practiced Chinese martial arts. There are several hundred forms of kung fu, but they share many basic principles.

Combination

It combines both soft and hard styles, mostly in the form of punches, kicks, strikes and blocks. Kung fu means "done well."

Wing Chun

Wing chun is one of the best-known styles of kung fu. It was developed as a soft style by a woman named Yim Wing Chun. Wing Chun literally means "eternal springtime." Wing chun kung fu focuses on the center of the body to conserve energy.

The Chinese refer to kung fu as their national martial art.

Close Range

Kung fu is practiced at very close range. This means that the attacks and the responses are very fast, and it takes a lot of practice to work at high speed.

Punches

Wing chun kung fu punches are very effective. They use a throwing action that develops a lot of power, even over a small distance.

Traditional kung fu is a way of attaining true development.

Animal Styles

Some moves are based on the actions of animals and birds. For instance, the crane uses a pecking action with the thumb and fingers, while the snake springs toward the opponent with a fast strike.

Kung Fu Monks

The Shaolin monks developed many different styles of kung fu. The styles developed as they were taught to villagers throughout China.

A Shaolin monk performing kung fu.

Kicks

All the kicks in wing chun kung fu are aimed at areas below the waist. This helps the kung fu artist to maintain balance.

Blocks

A kung fu block not only deflects an opponent's attack but prevents him from guarding against a response. This is called closing off.

Various forms of kickboxing have been practiced in China for thousands of years.

Styles

As the styles have developed and grown in popularity, they have introduced elements from other martial arts, including kung fu, tae kwon do, wrestling and western boxing. Kickboxing is practiced as a competitive sport. The two most popular forms are wu shu kwan and san shou.

Military Origin

The modern style of san shou was developed in the 1920s by the Chinese military. They wanted to create a practical form of defense that combined traditional martial arts philosophy with modern sports science and fitness.

Platform

Competitive san shou bouts take place on a platform — similar to a boxing ring without ropes. Competitors can score points by throwing their opponent from the platform!

Protection

The powerful kicks and punches used in kickboxing mean that protective gear must be worn. Padded headgear, gloves and shoes protect the kickboxer from their attacker.

Kickboxers can generate great power.

Sparring

Beginners will start with basic sparring. This involves learning how to throw and block simple kicks and punches.

Roundhouse

The high, spinning kick common to most forms of kickboxing is known as a roundhouse kick.

Sparring practice helps to develop timing, reaction coordination and intuition.

Takedowns

A kickboxer performing a roundhouse kick is in a vulnerable position. If alert, the opponent can sweep his leg away, causing a takedown.

Body Locks

Wrestling-style body locks are taught in many types of Chinese kickboxing. However, they are left out of competitive bouts so that the action is not interrupted.

Competitors use 10 oz. gloves for about 150 lbs. (68 kg) or less, and 12 oz. gloves for over 150 lbs. (68 kg).

The martial art of jeet kune do was developed by Bruce Lee — probably the world's most famous martial artist.

Bruce Lee

Bruce Lee had trained in kung fu and studied many other martial arts and combat fighting sports. He found the rules and discipline of these styles restrictive, so he developed jeet kune do — "the way of the intercepting fist."

Street Style

Lee found that the rules of martial arts did not take into account the realities of street fighting, making them less effective as a means of self-defense. His aim was to develop a style that would prove effective in combat against fighters who were not following any rules.

No Rules?

The philosophy behind jeet kune do is that the student must train hard, learn what he can, then use only the things that suit him best. Lee believed that you should use your opponent's technique to create your own, saying "Your action should be as fast as a shadow adapting to a moving object."

One Move

Jeet kune do emphasizes fluidity and efficiency of movement. For instance, rather than blocking and punching in two moves, the whole action is done in one move.

Attack

Unlike other martial arts, the approach of jeet kune do is that attack is the best form of defense.

Bruce Lee founded the discipline of jeet kune do.

Fighting Fit

Physical fitness is essential in jeet kune do as the artist must react quickly. Both physical and mental speed are vital, as the artist must process the action in his head faster than his opponent.

Inside and Out

The practice of jeet kune do combines the concepts of the internal soft styles, such as t'ai chi, with those of the external hard styles, such as kung fu.

JKD Today

Jeet kune do continues to be practiced in the way that Lee left it, but some practitioners have developed the style. Some military organizations and police forces train recruits in jeet kune do.

Jeet kune do is a self-defense-oriented martial art, using weapons (stick and knife).

T'ai chi is a popular form of the Chinese internal arts. It is based on the relationship between two opposing forces in nature, commonly described as yin and yang.

Taoist monks were first to practice the art of t'ai chi.

Calmness
T'ai chi combines relaxation and exercise in a series of continuous, flowing body movements. The art helps to cultivate a feeling of calmness.

Snake vs Crane
T'ai chi can be traced to a 12th-century Taoist monk named Chang San Fung. He created the art after seeing a fight between a snake and a crane.

Use the Force
T'ai chi is based on the principle of the soft overpowering the hard. In terms of combat, a t'ai chi artist will use his attacker's energy against him. Force is never met with force.

Inner Peace
The exercises associated with t'ai chi are also intended to promote a sense of well being within the practitioner.

T'ai chi is an exercise for relaxation, health and self-defense.

22

Healing Art

T'ai chi is commonly practiced to help treat medical conditions. It is thought it can help increase blood circulation and develop flexibility. The slow, graceful nature of t'ai chi makes it popular with the elderly.

Starting Out

Learning t'ai chi begins with basic methods of aligning the body and maintaining balance. Slow, precise movement is the basis of the art, although some styles also include explosively fast moves.

Lower Strength

T'ai chi focuses on the legs and hips as a source of strength. This helps keep the body in a state of relaxation.

Public Arts

In China, t'ai chi is often practiced by large groups of people in squares and other public places, usually early in the morning.

The postures of t'ai chi provide balance in the body.

Japanese Martial Arts

The Japanese martial arts date back more than 600 years. These arts, which are founded on the traditions of the ruling warrior classes, are known as koryu bujutso.

Tradition

Respect for others has always been an essential part of the martial arts. Modern Japanese styles have continued that tradition.

Ryu

Japanese martial arts are taught at schools called ryu. Most of these were created by noble samurai.

A Japanese samurai warrior.

Training Hall

Japanese martial arts are taught and practiced in a special training hall called a dojo. The dojo may differ according to the style being practiced. Where a lot of throwing takes place, as in judo, the dojo will have a padded floor.

Order and Respect

When entering and leaving the dojo, students must bow to the instructor. This is a sign of respect.

Students execute a standing bow (ritsu-rei) when entering and leaving the dojo, and at the start and end of a contest or practice.

Samurai

In ancient Japan, the samurai were a noble and respected class of warriors. For them, to die in battle was believed to guarantee life in the next world.

The samurai traditions are important in Japanese martial arts.

25

Kendo

Kendo — "the way of the sword" — is a Japanese weapon art, based upon the two-handed sword-fighting skills of the samurai.

History

Between the 14th and 16th centuries, sword skills were taught throughout Japan. The modern form of kendo was born in the 19th century and, by the 1950s, kendo had become part of the school curriculum.

Philosophy

Kendo emphasises mental and physical strength and builds character, self-discipline and respect. It is not practiced for self-defense.

Students of kendo.

Swords

Naturally, the use of real swords is very dangerous, so kendo uses a bamboo sword called a shinai. Kendo artists also wear a range of protective clothing, collectively known as bogu.

Headguard

The striking-looking headguard used in kendo is called a men. A scarf called a tenegui is worn inside the men. This cushions blows and soaks up sweat.

Breastplate

The body protector is made up of a very soft, flexible mune and a plastic or bamboo breastplate called a do.

Gloves

The gloves offer protection almost to the elbow. They are called kote.

Shirts and Skirts

A special jacket called a kendo-gi is worn beneath the body armor. Loose-fitting skirts called hakama allow freedom of movement. The hips are protected by tare.

Waza

The attack and defense movements in kendo are known as waza. To be successful, artists must focus on their stance and footwork, and the technique of their cuts and thrusts.

Scoring Cuts

Points are awarded in competition for hitting certain targets with the right technique. The targets are the men, do and kote.

Sword Technique

The correct technique involves using the left hand to power the sword and the right to control its direction.

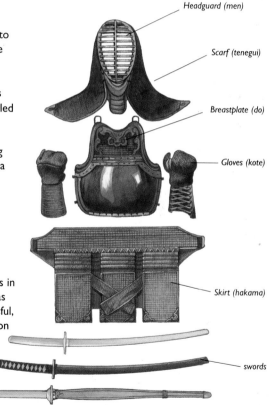

Headguard (men)

Scarf (tenegui)

Breastplate (do)

Gloves (kote)

Skirt (hakama)

swords

The Japanese martial art of ninjutsu has a somewhat mysterious and mystical nature.

Art of Stealth

Ninjutsu means "the art of stealth," and its early practitioners — ninjas — were experts in camouflage and secret undercover work. They were hired to carry out espionage (spying) and even contract killings. Such was the legendary status of the ninjas, it was widely believed that they were able to make themselves invisible.

Becoming Invisible

There are several tricks to moving without being seen but one of the most important is to breathe in time with the movement of

A Japanese ninja.

your body. Holding breath can cause muscle tension and may mean a noisy sharp intake of breath if you are startled.

Feuds and Families

Ninjutsu can be traced back to around 800 years ago, when the samurai were the ruling class in Japan. Ninjas often formed families, or clans, who did not want to serve the samurai.

Disguise

The ninjas were masters of disguise and were able to blend into a community, adapting to almost any situation.

Weapons

Ninjutsu features an astonishing range of weapons and equipment — more than any other martial art. These range from to ki — climbing equipment – to the hito washi, a type of board that, according to legend, enabled the ninja to hover above the ground.

The art of ninjutsu uses lethal weapons.

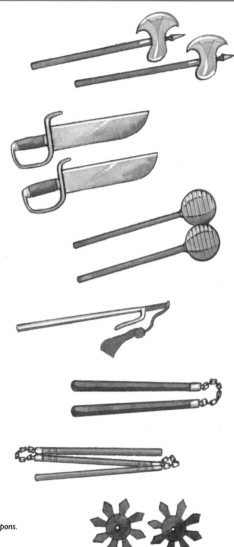

Judo is a very popular Japanese martial art based upon jujitsu. It was founded in 1882 by Dr. Jigro Kano, a university professor.

Origins

Dr. Kano took the less dangerous techniques of jujitsu and other styles and refined them to form the modern style of judo. It is a safe but effective martial art known for its impressive styles of throwing, grappling and striking.

Gentle Art

Judo means "gentle way" and, as such, is a good martial art for beginners and children. However, judo competitions still can be quite vigorous.

Falling

The first thing that a judo student is taught is how to fall properly. The body needs to be relaxed and the arms should take most of the shock of hitting the ground. This is known as breakfalling.

Throwing

The aim of judo is to trip or throw your opponent to the ground and, if necessary, hold him in that position. There are three basic throws, known collectively as nage.

Judo students must learn how to fall properly.

Striking

Striking moves, similar to those used in jujitsu, are still learned by some advanced judo artists. They are not permitted in competitive judo.

Grappling

Grappling, or groundwork, is known as katame. Once your opponent is on the ground, the aim is to hold him in that position for 30 seconds. The basic technique involves holding your arm around your opponent's neck and pressing your body weight against him.

Competitions

Points are awarded in judo competitions according to the quality of the throws and the groundwork. Tournaments, known as shiai, range from small events to the Olympic Games. Typically, competitors fight someone who has the same belt and is of a similar weight.

Belts

There are seven colored belts awarded according to skill level. The order of colors is white, yellow, orange, green, blue, brown and black. It takes years of practice to reach black belt.

Students must hold their opponents down for 30 seconds.

Aikido is a graceful Japanese martial art known as "the way of harmony." Its basic philosophy is that force is never met with force.

Avoiding Action

Instead of using force, avoiding action is taken and the attacker's own force is used against him. For this reason, it is an excellent form of self-defense and is taught by many police forces around the world.

Origins

Aikido was founded by Morehei Ueshiba in the early 20th century. He was an expert in jujitsu but wanted to create a means of defense that required little effort. Morehei Ueshiba is often called "O Sensei," meaning "Great Teacher."

Inner Energy

Learning aikido involves understanding the nature of an inner force known as ki. Control of this force can be used against your opponent.

Techniques

Although aikido is based on avoiding action, it does involve throws and locks taken from jujitsu and other throws taken from kenjutsu.

A student and master practice aikido.

Kata

Non-competitive aikido
is known as kata. In it
the nage (defender)
and the uke (attacker)
display a number of
moves of their choice
in a time limit.

Competitive Aikido

There are three forms
of competitive aikido.
Tanto randori is fought
over two rounds, with
the uke armed with
a rubber knife.
Randori kyoghi
is unarmed, while
ninindori features
three contestants.

*Randori kyoghi
is an unarmed
form of aikido.*

33

The islands of the Philippines are home to a distinctive style of martial arts.

Self-defense

There are several different types of Filipino martial arts — escrima, arnis and kali are the best-known. These are self-defense arts that use both empty-hand styles and weapon techniques. Dumog, sikaran and panantukan do not use any weapons. Filipino martial arts date from about the 9th century AD.

Simple Arts

Filipino martial arts were designed to be simple to learn. They were developed when the villages were under threat from invaders, and the people needed to learn quickly how to defend themselves.

Keep it Simple

The philosophy of simplicity remains today. Filipino martial arts are similar to Bruce Lee's jeet kune do, in that students are encouraged to work on the techniques that suit them best.

The use of one stick is called baston.

Weapons or Not

Many of the techniques that involve weapons are the same, or very similar to those that do not. This means that practitioners can adapt to different self-defense situations without needing to know lots of different techniques.

Triangles

The triangle is an important symbol in the Filipino martial arts. It represents strength, and many of the moves are based around a triangular pattern.

Live Hand

The live hand is an important concept in Filipino martial arts. It refers to the hand that does not contain the main weapon. It is used for checking, blocking, striking and to assist with disarming and locks.

Sticks

The use of sticks is central to most of the Filipino martial art styles. Baston involves the use of one stick. Two sticks used in a criss-cross style is called sinawali.

Uniforms

Unlike martial arts such as judo, there is no requirement to wear a uniform. Artists may wear T-shirts if they wish.

Shoes are always worn to protect the feet and re-create conditions of day-to-day life.

Belts

It is only recently, as FMA have become more popular, that a ranking system based on belts has been introduced.

Filipino martial arts do not require a uniform to be worn.

Filipino martial artists train with both weapons and empty hands.

Various forms of martial arts have been practiced for thousands of years in the part of Asia now divided into North and South Korea.

Origins

The Japanese troops that occupied the area during the early 20th century introduced karate, judo and kendo. Many new styles began to develop, among them hapkido, kuk sool won, hwa rang do and tae kwon do.

Hapkido

Hapkido combines joint locks, pressure points, throws, kicks and strikes for practical self-defense. It emphasizes circular motion and control of the opponent in a similar way to aikido.

The founder of hapkido was Yong Shul Choi, a Korean. It is likely that he was taken to work in Japan when he was a child.

Hwa Rang Do

Hwa rang do is a modern art, developed in the 1960s. It involves unarmed combat, weapon skills, internal training and healing techniques.

Kuk Sool Won

This style brings together parts of many traditional Korean styles. It focuses on mental and physical energy, along with meditation, acupuncture and breathing exercises. Kuk sool won involves more than 3,600 different techniques.

A heel kick in tae kwon do.

Training Hall

The training hall or school where Korean martial arts are taught is called the dojang, which translates as "school where the way is taught."

Etiquette

Etiquette plays an important role in Korean martial arts. When entering the dojang, the student should bow to the teacher. When the class is due to begin, the teacher will clap his hands, and once again the students should bow. Students are expected to be disciplined and respectful throughout the class.

Belts

As with other martial arts, there is a belt ranking system. In tae kwon do, the order is white, yellow, green, blue, red and black.

Black is the highest-ranking belt in tae kwon do.

Korean martial arts balance physical power with mental power.

Tae Kwon Do

Tae kwon do means "the way of the foot and the fist." It is similar in many ways to karate and is famous for its range and quality of kicks.

Olympic Sport

Tae kwon do was officially sponsored by the Korean government during the 1950s, and this led to the creation of a formal teaching and grading system. One of the most popular martial arts in the world, it became an Olympic sport in the year 2000.

General Choi

General Choi Hong Hi, an early pioneer of tae kwon do, is sometimes credited with naming the art. He formed the International Tae Kwon Do Federation (ITF) in 1966 to promote the art around the world.

Tae kwon do is famous for its kicks.

Sparring

Sparring involves two fighters practicing their techniques to develop timing, focus and speed. In competitive sparring, points are scored when certain targets are struck with the correct technique.

Etiquette

As with all martial arts, etiquette is important. The suit (dobok) should be clean, no jewelry should be worn, proper bows should be made on entering and exiting the dojang, and unless it is absolutely necessary, there should be no talking.

Patterns

A series of set techniques performed against an imaginary opponent is known as a pattern. One of the first patterns learnt is chon ji tul — the heaven and earth pattern.

Destruction

Practicing breaking objects, such as a piece of wood, is known as destruction. This helps focus the mind and develop the effectiveness of a technique.

ITF Tae Kwon Do

In ITF tae kwon do competitions, the participants carry out low-impact attacks wearing head, fist and foot protection.

Olympic/WTF Tae Kwon Do

The form of tae kwon do performed at the Olympics is a much more physical style. Full power kicks and punches to the head and body are allowed, though punches to the face are not. Protective headgear is worn.

Right middle section snap kick.

Tang soo do is a classic Korean martial art. It means "way of the Tang hand," after the styles developed under the Tang dynasty in China.

Combination

Tang soo do is a combination of hard and soft styles with some soft, flowing movements. It uses a lot of foot techniques and is famous for its range of spectacular kicks.

Non-competitive

Tang soo do is a martial art in the classical sense: it is not a sport as such. Its main purpose is to improve and focus the emotions and spirit of those who practice it.

Tang soo do combines hard and soft styles.

Protection

Early versions of tang soo do have been traced to nearly 2,000 years ago. Originally people learned tang soo do to protect themselves from the samurai.

Strength is demonstrated through the breaking of boards.

Benefits

The physical benefits you can expect from taking part in tang soo do include improved posture, flexibility and stamina. Tang soo do also aims to teach concentration, self-discipline and self-respect.

Board Breaking

As in tae kwon do, the power of a technique is demonstrated by smashing plastic boards.

Tang soo do is known for its flying, jumping and spinning kicks.

Five Principles

All students of tang soo do must follow five basic principles:

1. Loyalty to one's monarch and country
2. Obedience to parents and elders
3. Respect to instructors and seniors
4. Self-control
5. Proper use of one's art

The world of martial arts has some mysterious and unusual traditions.

Out of Practice

Arts such as karate, judo and tae kwon do are very widely practiced and quite familiar, but there are some little-known styles that are so strange or so dangerous that they are no longer practiced.

Monkey Kung Fu

Known variously as tai sing mun, ta sheng or dai shing pop gar, monkey kung fu is considered to be one of the strangest of all the martial arts. It is full of rolling and twisting movements, which are intended to confuse the opponent. Then a powerful kicking attack is made.

Kung Fu Styles

Other unusual kung fu styles include mantis kung fu, based on the attacking and defending techniques of the bird, and northern Shaolin kung fu, a long-fist technique that stresses the importance of kicking rather than hand techniques.

Head Butt

Pachigi is a somewhat bizarre martial art from Korea. The basic style involves opponents head-butting one another — not recommended!

Kobujutsu

Kobujutsu, like karate, began on the Japanese island of Okinawa. The style of kobujutsu uses weapons such as the walking stick and the rice grinding handle.

Capoeira is a mixture of cartwheels, handstands, flips and spinning kicks.

Bone Breaking

Lua is a fabled martial art from the Pacific island of Hawaii. Its practitioners were said to be able to break the bones of their opponents without the use of weapons.

Extinct

Lua used the manipulation of pressure points to dislocate and break bones. Fortunately it is now extinct.

Dancing Art

Capoeira is a Brazilian martial art, that appears very much like a form of dance. It is performed to music and is today essentially a form of entertainment.

Danger Dance

Despite appearances, capoeira is very dangerous, as rapid kicks are delivered to the head — one of the most important parts of the body.

Capoeira uses incredible movements.

Martial arts movies have singlehandedly increased interest in the arts outside of Asia.

Most of the martial arts superstars were very accomplished artists before becoming movie stars and some of them, such as Bruce Lee, developed their own styles and philosophies.

Bruce Lee

Bruce Lee was the original martial arts superstar. He is often said to be responsible for raising the profile of martial arts around the world. He died in 1973, the year his famous film *Enter the Dragon* was released.

Underdog

Lee was short and skinny, but his awesome kung fu skills made him unbeatable. He always appeared to be the underdog. This probably helped to make his films so successful.

Jackie Chan

Jackie Chan studied a number of martial arts, notably kung fu and hapkido, and made his name as a stuntman in Hong Kong-produced kung fu movies.

Hollywood Star

After appearing in the Bruce Lee movies *Fist of Fury* and *Enter the Dragon*, Chan moved to the United States where he has since become a major Hollywood star. His films are noted for their speed and comic touches.

Bruce Lee

Jackie Chan

Chuck Norris

Chuck Norris, who starred in several action movies throughout the 1970s, 1980s and 1990s, started out as a karate and tang soo do champion. He made his breakthrough in Bruce Lee's *Return of the Dragon*.

Jean-Claude Van Damme

Jean-Claude Van Damme has starred in a number of martial arts movies, including *No Retreat, No Surrender* and *Kickboxer*. Van Damme had studied karate since the age of 10, becoming European middleweight champion before moving into films.

Chuck Norris

Jet Li

Jet Li trained extensively in Shaolin and wu shu kung fu. He is credited with rekindling the interest in martial arts during the 1980s. Li has starred in several Hollywood movies, including *Lethal Weapon 4* and *Romeo Must Die*.

The Karate Kid

Ralph Macchio starred as *The Karate Kid* in 1984, as a victim of bullying who learns karate. Not only does his new skill help him to take on the bullies but also he learns that there is more to martial arts than fighting.

The Magnificent Seven

The classic holiday movie, *The Magnificent Seven*, was based on a Japanese film, *The Seven Samurai*, about warriors defending a village from bandits.

Jet Li

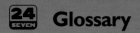

Here you will find the styles and country of origin of all the martial arts styles mentioned in this book.

China

Dai shing pop gar	monkey kung fu — empty-hand, hard, external
Fusing-i chuan	soft, internal
Hsing i	soft, internal
Jeet kune do	empty-hand, soft/hard, external/internal
Kung fu	empty-hand, soft/hard, external/internal
Pa kua	empty-hand, soft, internal
San shou	type of Chinese kickboxing — hard, external
Shaolin	type of kung fu — empty-hand, hard, external
T'ai chi	empty-hand, soft, internal
Ta sheng	monkey kung fu — empty-hand, hard, external
Tai sing mun	monkey kung fu — empty-hand, hard, external
Wing chun	type of kung fu — empty-hand, hard, external
Wu shu kwan	type of Chinese kickboxing — hard, external

Judo is a Japanese art.

Japan

Aikido	empty-hand, hard, external
Iaido	weapon art, soft, internal
Judo	empty-hand, soft, external
Jujitsu	empty-hand, soft, external
Karate	empty-hand, hard, external
Kobujutsu	weapon art, hard, external
Kendo	weapon art, hard, external
Kyudo	weapon art, soft, internal
Ninjutsu	weapon art/empty-hand, soft/hard, internal/external
Shorinji kempo	empty-hand, hard, external

Korea

Hapkido	empty-hand, hard, external
Hwa rang do	empty-hand, hard, external
Kuk sool won	empty-hand, hard, external
Pachigi	empty-hand, hard, external
Tae kwon do	empty-hand, hard, external
Tang soo do	empty-hand, hard, external

Philippines

Arnis	weapon art, hard, external
Escrima	weapon art, hard, external
Kali	weapon art, hard, external

You can find out more about martial arts on the Internet. Ask an adult to help you check out the sites below:

www.ijf.org
The website of the International Judo Federation.

www.itatkd.com
The website for the International Tae Kwon Do Association.

www.itka-karate.com
The website of the International Traditional Karate Federation, the governing body of traditional karate.

Picture Credits
The publisher would like to thank the following contacts and organizations for their involvement, help and cooperation in creating this project:

• The students of **Hollesley Judo Club** and **Ho Wan Kung Fu Academy**;

Photos: Chinese kickboxing, tang soo do lua, escrima, kali, jujitsu, iaido, hapkido, kuk sool won, jeet kune do.

• **All Star Picture Library**: photos of Jet Li, Chuck Norris, Bruce Lee, Jackie Chan;

• **Getty Images**: photo of Taoist monk;

• **Action Plus**: tai chi (Neale Haynes) Shaolin kung fu (Glyn Kirk), tae kwon do (Tony Henshaw), kendo (Mile Hewitt), kickboxing (Neil Tingle), aikido (J M emportes/DPPI), capoeira (Franck Faugere/DPPI).